The
WISEST WISDOM

300 quotes for life

Written by Zachery McGivens

Introduction:

This book is dedicated to all those people that have unselfishly helped, motivated and inspired myself and others to do great things. I've had a lot of help in my life and I want to pay it forward. Sometimes navigating through life can be difficult. I want to help people by providing some of useful insight but I wanted to do it in my own way. To the reader you've made a great decision purchasing this book, Congratulations! I've been called a creative genius, told that I have a beautiful mind, and considered to be one of the greatest philosophers of our time, all true statements by the way. I wanted to write a book that is direct and to the point, no fluff just great content that you can read on the go, at anytime. "THE WISEST WISDOM" is a collection of 300 original quotes that I've come up with, at least as far as I know they are. This book contains thought provoking gems, inspirational words of encouragement and enlightening pearls of wisdom that will expand your mind. This is an invaluable resource you have here, I mean that. This book is like a Swiss army knife. Just pick a page and it's going to contain a functional tool for life. By the way this is a very easy book to read, even people that don't typically like to read books will discover that they enjoy reading this one. For the best results please read at least of page of this book everyday. The repetition is key. I consider this to be a truly wonderful work of literary art. One might say it's the Mona Lisa of books. Trust me they don't teach you this stuff in school. This is some deep, next level stuff here people. Quite simply put, it's a revelation. Let's get started.

1. "We only listen to what we wanna do or believe." - Mchezo Bwana

2. "Don't ever offer help to people that don't want it and that aren't willing to help themselves." - Mchezo Bwana

3. "Trauma is difficult to recover from because we try so hard to hide it. When we develop the courage to honesty face it we can be healed." - Mchezo Bwana

4. "If you want to lose weight you have to be willing to make a habit of thinking positive, exercising and eating right." - Mchezo Bwana

5. "Sometimes you'll have to choose between hanging around certain people or success. That should be an easy decision." - Mchezo Bwana

6. "Shared experiences help to strengthen a bond." - Mchezo Bwana

7. "You're ready to show your idea when you have it written out." - Mchezo Bwana

8. "You admit your guilt when you have to lie about your deeds." - Mchezo Bwana

9. "Never be fooled by a smile." - Mchezo Bwana

10. "One must be great at lying to their-self to become good at lying to someone else." - Mchezo Bwana

11. "Emotional thinking causes us to ignore the signs, even though we may see them. And then, later on when it goes bad, we act like we didn't have a clue. Don't ignore the signs respond to them correctly." - Mchezo Bwana

12. "Words can be used to deceive but actions and results are verifiable." - Mchezo Bwana

13. "When someone tells you that you should do this or you should do that, ask that person if they can show you how it's done and then see what they say." - Mchezo Bwana

14. "We all have something positive to contribute to the world. So what are you giving?" - Mchezo Bwana

15. "If you think you can only achieve so much before hitting a glass ceiling it's only because you allow it to remain there." - Mchezo Bwana

16. "When you think about your future it should give you a reason to smile." - Mchezo Bwana

17. "Admit that you don't know everything and there's a chance that you may become enlightened." - Mchezo Bwana

18. "People that can't handle the truth will try so hard to hold onto lies." - Mchezo Bwana

19. "Be ready for anything, make sure you're on your toes like Baryshnikov and the Flintstones." - "Mchezo Bwana

20. "If you spend your lifetime learning and adding new skills you'll never get bored." - Mchezo Bwana

21. "When you refuse to do for self you become dependent on someone else." - Mchezo Bwana

22. "The key to being cool is to be relaxed." - Mchezo Bwana

23. "Don't stay down pick yourself up. Whenever you fall, bounce back up like a basketball." - Mchezo Bwana

24. "The agreeable person is the one you make moves with. The disagreeable people are who you'll get stuck with." - Mchezo Bwana

25. "If you want it done then you'll need to force yourself to do it or you may waste even more time waiting for someone else to do it for you." - Mchezo Bwana

26. "You can't make someone listen if they don't want to hear it." - Mchezo Bwana

27. "Being grateful gives you more things to appreciate." - Mchezo Bwana

28. "I pray that anyone who has lost a loved one finds peace and that they will do the same for someone else in a similar situation." - Mchezo Bwana

29. "When you believe in yourself there are no limits." - Mchezo Bwana

30. "Pressure is like an X-ray machine being under it displays what's really in you." - Mchezo Bwana

31. "Leave 'em where they're at if they don't want to get on board. You gotta truckin' on." - Mchezo Bwana

32. "Two things about sells is asking questions and making suggestions." - Mchezo Bwana

33. "Having a conversation with a person that is unwilling to change their mind is a like playing duck duck goose, you'll just keep running in circles." - Mchezo Bwana

34. "The more you pay attention, the fewer things get missed." - Mchezo Bwana

35. "When you know how something operates you have insight on how to control it." -Mchezo Bwana

36. "To be first get there early and sometimes you'll need to stay late." - Mchezo Bwana

37. "Repetition is the key. The more you read, watch, listen and do something, the more your awareness expands." - Mchezo Bwana

38. "Our imagination is our greatest gift, when we utilize it we can achieve our dreams." - Mchezo Bwana

39. "Anybody can be great but not everyone is willing to do what it takes. Belief and action are what will make the difference." - Mchezo Bwana

40. "If you need directions don't be afraid to ask somebody for help, just make sure it's from someone that has already been where you want to go." - Mchezo Bwana

41. "The question your company should be asking is; How can we make the customer experience better?" - Mchezo Bwana

42. "Being prepared is like getting a heads up before a future event. You're ready for what's going to happen in advance. It's a spoiler alert." - Mchezo Bwana

43. "When you're seen with a celebrity people start to think that you're important and when people think that you're important they'll want to be seen with you." - Mchezo Bwana

44. "When we resist doing what we must it delays us from getting the things that we want." - Mchezo Bwana

45. "Nosey people want to know something they can gossip about." - Mchezo Bwana

46. "Let go of those negative thoughts and more positive things will come into your life. Hold onto those negative thoughts you'll likely remain frustrated." - Mchezo Bwana

47. "The money is in Motivation." - Mchezo Bwana

48. "Only tell people the things that you don't mind them gossiping about." - Mchezo Bwana

49. "Procrastinate and you're already late." - Mchezo Mchezo

50. "Limit any negative distractions by immediately focusing you attention on something more positive. You should be in control of what you think about." - Mchezo Bwana

51. "If you believe that you are less than someone else, it's only because you've allowed yourself to be convinced." - Mchezo Bwana

52. "It may not be a comfortable road to success but you'll feel a whole lot better when you get there." - Mchezo Bwana

53. "You wanna win? Then team up with the winners. You've got to cut the losers." - Mchezo Bwana

54. "We do things that we know are bad for us because they make us feel good and we lack the discipline to stop doing them." - Mchezo Bwana

55. "Doing the hard things are relatively easy to do. The difference is often that one person is willing to step out of their comfort zone and do what needs to be done in order to be successful, while the unsuccessful person isn't willing to do it." - Mchezo Bwana

56. "Excuses are usually the lies we tell, in order to make ourselves feel better about why something didn't happen." - Mchezo Bwana

58. "It's easier to feel sorry for yourself than to do for self." - Mchezo Bwana

57. "Practicing what you preach and taking your own advice are two things that would instantly improve the world, if everyone was really true to their word." - Mchezo Bwana

59. "You'll need to ask for help when you can't do it alone." - Mchezo Bwana

60. "Don't tell a weak person your business, they'll fold quicker than a poker player with a bad hand." - Mchezo Bwana

61. "If you need experience or want a free education, start volunteering." - Mchezo Bwana

62. "It ain't over 'till it's double zeros on the clock." - Mchezo Bwana

63. "We may ask for something that we didn't really want but it may turn out to be what we really needed in order to grow." - Mchezo Bwana

64. "Fear; it's ruined more dreams than an alarm clock." - Mchezo Bwana

65. "If someone is making you feel bad there's probably something wrong with how you're handling the situation." - Mchezo Bwana

66. "In my opinion the world needs more brave thinkers and innovators that want to make our planet a better place." - Mchezo Bwana

67. "Self limiting thoughts are caused by our environment, beliefs, and conditioning. The good news is that all of them can be positively altered for our benefit to create a new thought habit that is infinite in potential." - Mchezo Bwana

68. "Changing a negative habit takes a commitment to yourself, a whole lot of effort and even more patience." - Mchezo Bwana

69. "The best thing about memories are their ability to allow us to revisit those happy moments and emotions again." - Mchezo Bwana

70. "Find a common cause, negotiate a win win for everyone involved and execute the game plan. Then everyone should be happy." - Mchezo Bwana

71. "A positive message is the best one to spread."- Mchezo Bwana

72. "Comfortable conditions can make you complacent, unpleasant conditions can get you motivated." - Mchezo Bwana

73. "When you can admit when you're wrong, you're doing something right." - Mchezo Bwana

74. "It's selfish to cage a bird, real love is letting it be free." - Mchezo Bwana

75. "Truth is the archenemy of hate." - Mchezo Bwana

76. "Most people don't think, they just believe they do." - Mchezo Bwana

77. "If you want to improve your situation you must be willing to improve yourself." - Mchezo Bwana

78. "When you're impatient it seems to take longer to get there. I've found that looking for shortcuts had cost me more time than going the long route." - Mchezo Bwana

79. "If you want to get motivated listen to a motivational speaker, if you want to get inspired listen to an inspirational speaker if you want to feel depressed, watch the news." - Mchezo Bwana

80. "Resist the urge to quit just because the road may be long and difficult. Stay strong." - Mchezo Bwana

81. "Most people assume what they don't know." - Mchezo Bwana

82. "You may have to pay a fee to meet that person you should probably see." - Mchezo Bwana

83. "It would be foolish to assume that you know more than someone else. We all know something that no one else knows." - Mchezo Bwana

84. "The best way to show gratitude is by giving it your all." - Mchezo Bwana

85. When we speak words that we later regret, the feeling is like getting a Christmas gift that you hate and you don't the receipt. Oh, how we wish so much that we could take them back." - Mchezo Bwana

86. "You don't know how someone will receive the information until it's given to them." - Mchezo Bwana

87. "Better to have a small circle of great friends than to hang around a large group that ain't ." - Mchezo Bwana

88. "Sheep look to the shepherd. Leaders look for examples." - Mchezo Bwana

89. "The people you are around can lift you up or bring you down if you let them." - Mchezo Bwana

90. "The three root motivations of hate; 3. Jealousy, 2. Insecurity 1. Fear." - Mchezo Bwana

91. "You have to put your focus in the right place in order to get what you really want." - Mchezo Bwana

92. "Before you go to do something consider asking yourself this question; If I do this will it get me closer to my goal? If the answer is no, do something else." - Mchezo Bwana

93. "Trying to have the last word may just keep the conversation going. Let the other person have it. Say no more and it's over." - Mchezo Bwana

94. "If you have to lie to get what you want, once the truth comes out, you'll most likely lose it." - Mchezo Bwana

95. "Don't expect for something to be given to you if you aren't willing to ask for it." - Mchezo Bwana

96. "Being concerned about what other people thought about me was one of the biggest mistakes I ever made because I was holding myself back." - Mchezo Bwana

97. "We pay more for quality because we get more value." - Mchezo Bwana

98. "Give excuses the deuces." - Mchezo Bwana

99. "Results are like an alibi, because they're a clear statement made about what you were doing with your time." - Mchezo Bwana

100. "Laughter is the sound of happiness or ignorance." - Mchezo Bwana

101. "When you're direct and to the point you'll save yourself a lot of time." - Mchezo Bwana

102. "Spectators watch the players in the game." - Mchezo Bwana

103. "Achieving your goal is a 3 step process; Visualize, mobilize, actualize." - Mchezo Bwana

104. "When someone is disagreeable conversations should be minimal." - Mchezo Bwana

105. "Acknowledge the talent that you see in others. When people see something in us that we may not have seen in ourselves it gives us confidence. We begin to believe that we can achieve great things. It can really make a difference in someone's life." - Mchezo Bwana

106. "It's your dream, make it a reality. Some people are going to criticize you. So what, if you're doing good wouldn't you like to be happy." - Mchezo Bwana

107. "Worry about what you can control, which are your thoughts and actions." - Mchezo Bwana

108. "The threat of losing money can cause some people to remain silent and do things they really don't want to do." - Mchezo Bwana

109. "Words have more meaning to those that understand them." - Mchezo Bwana

110. "The desire for instant gratification can lead to procrastination." - Mchezo Bwana

111. "We all have different perspectives and with a little empathy we may better understand each other." - Mchezo Bwana

112. "Talking down to people isn't how you lift them up." - Mchezo Bwana

113. "No one has all the answers but somebody has one." - Mchezo Bwana

114. "If you want to blend in camouflage will help keep you from being seen." - Mchezo Bwana

115. "If you have to lie about it, you don't truly believe it." - Mchezo Bwana

116. "You only hang around negative people when you want to be criticized, made fun of, get your confidence bruised, doubted, disrespected, drained of enthusiasm and unproductive. Other than that you might have a little fun." - Mchezo Bwana

117. "Your demons are those negative thoughts and bad habits that you continue to hold on to." - Mchezo Bwana

118. "The difference between can and can't is your willingness to attempt it." - Mchezo Bwana

119. "Intent needs action to be realized." - Mchezo Bwana

120. "You'll see that opportunities are everywhere, if you just keep your eyes open." - Mchezo Bwana

121. "The television is not your friend it's your conditioner." - Mchezo Bwana

122. "There is no shortage of money, there's enough for everyone. So why so much jealousy and greed?" - Mchezo Bwana

123. "Let people be them and you be you especially if it doesn't effect anything that you do." - Mchezo Bwana

124. "When you're balanced you don't get too high or low." - Mchezo Bwana

125. "A great leader knows how to get their team to respond with a positive action." - Mchezo Bwana

126. "When doubt enters your mind make sure it has a quick exit." - Mchezo Bwana

127. "When you're insecure you're unsure, there's confidence in knowing." - Mchezo Bwana

128. "To become disciplined is a test to see what you're made of and how bad you really want it." - Mchezo Bwana

129. "You have to keep moving forward to prevent going backwards or becoming stagnant." - Mchezo Bwana

130. "Discipline is like a sleazy massage parlor, you have to pay for it up front but you do get a happy ending." - Mchezo Bwana

131. "Sometimes the struggle is simply feeling uncomfortable because your doing something you don't want to do." - Mchezo Bwana

132. "Let go of all the negativity, resentment, hate, fear, doubt, jealously, lies, insecurity, regret and anger because none of them can really make you happy." - Mchezo Bwana

133. "Being honest and true to yourself is as real as it gets." - Mchezo Bwana

134. "Most new discoveries were already known a long time ago." - Mchezo Bwana

135. "Trying to save everyone is unnecessary, everybody don't wanna be saved." - Mchezo Bwana

136. "When you take lots of notes you give yourself a reference to go back." - Mchezo Bwana

137. "When we are focused there's action, if we get distracted we become unproductive." - Mchezo Bwana

138. "Empathizing with someone else can be tough when you've never known the feeling." - Mchezo Bwana

139. "Go after what you want if it's really what you want no matter how nervous it makes you." - Mchezo Bwana

140. "The proper advice can change the direction of your life." - Mchezo Bwana

141. "It's tough to take a loss. Losing doesn't feel good but look at the bright side you should've learned a valuable lesson from it." - Mchezo Bwana

142. "Let more positive and confident thoughts occupy you mind." - Mchezo Bwana

143. "We waste our time and energy when we choose to be insecure about things that don't really matter to someone else." - Mchezo Bwana

144. "The people that want Governments are the people that don't want to take responsibility." - Mchezo Bwana

145. "Confidence conquers insecurity." - Mchezo Bwana

146. "Do you realize how much time and energy you'll waste arguing with people that aren't seeking to understand you and that don't want to get it?" - Mchezo Bwana

147. "Placebos are a testament to the minds ability to heal the body." - Mchezo Bwana

148. "Today is what we have to utilize. Invest in today. It's free. It's priceless." - Mchezo Bwana

149. "Your example is the best way to teach someone." - Mchezo Bwana

150. "Things are scary in those moments that we lack understanding. When we gain understanding and put things in proper perspective the fear subsides." - Mchezo Bwana

151. "Be you, be who you are and be free." - Mchezo Bwana

152. "Don't take the bait or you may end up like the fish." - Mchezo Bwana

153. "Insecure people lie the most." - Mchezo Bwana

154. "Don't live in the past, learn from it. Let go of regret. Forgive yourself. Begin again." - Mchezo Bwana

155. "When they start talking about it's impossible or it can't be done, then they can't be around me." - Mchezo Bwana

156. "Anyone that would rather compete against you rather than eat with you is really playing for the opposition." - Mchezo Bwana

157. "If you're disciplined and persistent the date may be uncertain but you will succeed." - Mchezo Bwana

158. "The wise don't rush to judgement, especially not before gathering information." - Mchezo Bwana

159. "If you fall down into a pit you can start praying and wait or you can pray and start climbing." - Mchezo Bwana

160. "Observation is more powerful than your opinion. Pay attention to what you see without bias. Respond logically not emotionally. If your intuition tells you something isn't right just walk away from that situation and find a better one." - Mchezo Bwana

161. "All things love praise, kids, animals, plants, water, the sun, God etc." - Mchezo Bwana

162. "As you become successful don't be surprised when some of your so called friends and relatives aren't very supportive, they may even try to sabotage your success. Some may think they've been passed up which causes them to feel insecure about themselves." - Mchezo Bwana

163. "It's much easier to lie to yourself than to face the truth. Being honest with yourself takes way more effort and usually requires you to change your behavior." - Mchezo Bwana

164. "You're success is a haters karma." - Mchezo Bwana

165. "The only thing worse than being disciplined is being broke. I try to remind myself of that fact whenever I start to lose focus." - Mchezo Bwana

166. "Avoid miserable people like you're playing a game of tag and they're it." - Mchezo Bwana

167. "You can't afford to be lazy if you want to be rich." - Mchezo Bwana

168. "Ignorance gets us lost, knowledge gives us a way forward." - Mchezo Bwana

169. "Do yourself a favor and be yourself, find your purpose, get over your insecurities and live the life of your dreams." - Mchezo Bwana

170. "We all want it to be easy but we don't always get our wish." - Mchezo Bwana

171. "Self doubt is one of the cruelest tricks of the devil, meant to hold you back from getting what you desire and being your true self. You must always reinforce the belief in yourself and your abilities in order to defeat this enemy." - Mchezo Bwana

172. "You get rewarded when you are disciplined." - Mchezo Bwana

173. "Whenever you start to feel like you don't have what it takes, understand that voice is doubt trying to sell you a lie, don't buy it." - Mchezo Bwana

174. "Even if you don't know what you're talking about, if you make it sound good enough somebody will buy it." - Mchezo Bwana

175. "The conversations you have say a lot about you." - Mchezo Bwana

176. "The only one that truly knows what you are capable of is our Creator." - Mchezo Bwana

177. "Just because they smile in your face does not mean they're your friend. Some people pretend like they want to see you win." - Mchezo Bwana

178. "If you want to be in a positive environment you have to be willing to remove yourself from a negative one." - Mchezo Bwana

179. "Behavior is learned. So who are you emulating? Are you proud of your behavior? Would you want someone else emulating you? Be honest with yourself." - Mchezo Bwana

180. "Give words of encouragement to those that you want to see do better." - Mchezo Bwana

181. "Eagles are a national symbol of greatness. Chickens are lunch. I know which one I'd rather be." - Mchezo Bwana

182. "Don't let anyone talk you into a situation that you don't really want to be in. You may regret it." - Mchezo Bwana

183. "Ask "Why" over and over and over again, until you know the solution." - Mchezo Bwana

184. "Be as great as you think you are. Be as great as you say you are. Be as great as you want to be." - Mchezo Bwana

185. "The best place to see the view is from the top." - Mchezo Bwana

186. "Good leaders know how to define roles, allocate task and utilize strengths." - Mchezo Bwana

187. "You can offer people something that no one else can." - Mchezo Bwana

188. "Look for validation outside of yourself and risk not being validated by someone else, for their own reasons." - Mchezo Bwana

189. "I don't need you to sugarcoat the truth just show me the proof." - Mchezo Bwana

190. "If you don't really want a person in your life, just be polite and move on." - Mchezo Bwana

191. "To take responsibility is to accept no excuses." - Mchezo Bwana

192. "Jealousy and insecurity can prevent some people from seeing an opportunity." - Mchezo Bwana

193. "The two best times to give advice are when it's asked for or paid for." -Mchezo Bwana"

194. "Be confident you can put yourself in a better situation. Have faith and know that." - Mchezo Bwana

195. "One more way the Universe communicates with you is through music." - Mchezo Bwana

196. "Build a strong team around you, because you're going to need one." - Mchezo Bwana

197. "When you take the time to do it correctly you don't have to worry about getting it wrong." - Mchezo Bwana

198. "Do things that make you uncomfortable, conquer your fears and you'll grow stronger." - Mchezo Bwana

199. "Don't hide your talents, our talents are gifts meant to be shared with others." - Mchezo Bwana

200. "You're more likely to do something if you write it down and set reminders for yourself." - Mchezo Bwana

201. "Cowardice is the ultimate form of selfishness." - Mchezo Bwana

202. "To help someone is to collaborate." - Mchezo Bwana

203. "When I started listening to good advice I started getting better results." - Mchezo Bwana

204. "When we set limits on ourselves, theres only so much we can do." - Mchezo Bwana

205. "Those too afraid to stand alone find comfort among the sheep." - Mchezo Bwana

206. "Following the crowd never really got me anywhere but with the rest of the crowd, I've accomplished more in life by being myself." - Mchezo Bwana

207. "A good parent encourages and disciplines." - Mchezo Bwana

208. "It's important to research history on your own and juxtapose the information. I've found that not everything we've been told is true." - Mchezo Bwana

209. "Getting organized creates more time, space and productivity." - Mchezo Bwana

210. "If someone isn't happy for you're success, they can't be trusted." - Mchezo Bwana

211. "It's a blessing to have people around you that know how to effectively encourage and motivate you especially during tough times. That is the type of environment you want to be in." - Mchezo Bwana

212. "Knowledge is supposed to be passed like a baton but sometimes the jealous and the greedy choose to be stingy with it." - Mchezo Bwana

213. "Do the thing that's going to get you the best result in the least amount of time and you can build momentum from that." - Mchezo Bwana

214. "Lead with logic. Logical thinking always produces a better way." - Mchezo Bwana

215. "You wanna know if someone should remain in your life? Ask them if they wouldn't mind supporting you by purchasing your product. Then you'll get your answer." - Mchezo Bwana

216. "The images we see are important because they provide us with a reference for what we can be." - Mchezo Bwana

217. "Take an inventory of the people in your life. Who's an asset, who's a liability?" - Mchezo Bwana

218. "It's easier to communicate with someone when you're speaking their language." - Mchezo Bwana

219. "Time does not wait for indecision." - Mchezo Bwana

220. "To sacrifice is difficult when it's something we don't want to give up, like doughnuts and candy." - Mchezo Bwana

221. "If you couldn't talk about it unless you were really about it, a lot of people would just be quiet." - Mchezo Bwana

222. "Don't depend on inconsistent people, they'll disappoint you." - Mchezo Bwana

223. "The most polite person in an interaction is the most difficult to make upset because they are the person most in control of their emotions." - Mchezo Bwana

224. "Sometimes the truth is like a pimple, it's in your face but you don't want to see it. So you try to cover it up yet it never seems to want to go away." - Mchezo Bwana

225. "You'll find high quality people when you look in better places." - Mchezo Bwana

226. "If you want someone's loyalty, give them food, money and security." - Mchezo Bwana

227. "There won't be an excuse if you don't make one up." - Mchezo Bwana

228. "The atheist isn't learned, more studying is required." - Mchezo Bwana

229. "Ask as many questions as possible in order to gain clarity." - Mchezo Bwana

230. "When you take responsibility for your actions you know who to hold accountable." - Mchezo Bwana

231. "The more you practice shooting the more confidence you'll have in your shot." - Mchezo Bwana

232. "Doing what you said you would do gives you credibility. Doing the opposite ruins your reputation." - Mchezo Bwana

233. "Achieving your dream is a haters nightmare, so make sure they have to sleep under the covers with the lights on." - Mchezo Bwana

234. "With every new day there is an opportunity for you to do something great." - Mchezo Bwana

235. "Jealousy is the fear of losing something that you desire and an acknowledgement that you perceive you lack something that someone else has." - Mchezo Bwana

236. "If you don't call out negative behavior it will continue." - Mchezo Bwana

237. "If it's up for interpretation it hasn't been clearly stated." - Mchezo Bwana

238. "The annoying thing about doubt is that it always seems to come at the worst possible time, when you're trying to accomplish something." - Mchezo Bwana

239. "If someone is not willing to take a step forward with you, they cannot go any further with you." - Mchezo Bwana

240. "The haters will try to deceive and distract you. They'll try to waste your time if you let them. Be aware and stay focused. Maneuver around them and play to win." - Mchezo Bwana

241. "When you're self-educated you have access to an unlimited amount of knowledge, in school they only teach you what they want you to know." - Mchezo Bwana

242. "Why worry about the opinion that someone else may have of you when you don't even know what they think of themselves." - Mchezo Bwana

243. "Credibility is earned not automatically given. Past deeds determine if someone deserves the benefit of the doubt, not a denial." - Mchezo Bwana

244. "Wherever you find excuses, denial is very near by." - Mchezo Bwana

245. "You have to be better than your competition if you want to beat them." - Mchezo Bwana

246. "Denial is like getting stuck in bumper to bumper rush hour traffic, very little progress is being made while you're in it." - Mchezo Bwana

247. "People are more likely to tell you what they believe rather than what they can prove." - Mchezo Bwana

248. "Time is precious, be grateful for the moment because it quickly becomes a memory." - Mchezo Bwana

249. "Some people still get it wrong even when the answer has been given to them." - Mchezo Bwana

250. "As a parent your job is to prepare your child for what they may face in life and how they should effectively navigate those situations." - Mchezo Bwana

251. "If you know what it takes but you're still not taking action you're most likely thinking of excuses why you shouldn't do it." - Mchezo Bwana

252. "You wanna win an argument? Present evidence." - Mchezo Bwana

253. "I'd rather get dunked on attempting a block than to never jump at all." - Mchezo Bwana

254. "If you want to be successful, use the strategies that have already been proven to work." - Mchezo Bwana

255. "In life you must be confident enough to walk alone if you want to reach your goal." - Mchezo Bwana

256. "Most people wear a mask everyday, Halloween is the one day that we choose to acknowledge it." - Mchezo Bwana

257. "For some people doing the right thing is difficult, for others, it may be too difficult." - Mchezo Bwana

258. "The ability to block out distractions for long periods of time is key to staying focused." - Mchezo Bwana

259. "Focus on what you dream of and what you love. Everything else is a distraction." - Mchezo Bwana

260. "If you want to understand women you have to know how they think." - Mchezo Bwana

261. "Don't live in the past with regret, forgive yourself, move forward, do good and be great." - Mchezo Bwana

262. "To be brave is to be in the minority, to conform is to be one of the masses." - Mchezo Bwana

263. "Invest your money in knowledge to acquire new skills and you'll earn even more in return." - Mchezo Bwana

264. "Ignorant people can be a danger to themselves and others whether they know it or not." - Mchezo Bwana

265. "If they ain't trying to assist, they should be dismissed." - Mchezo Bwana

266. "Being around positive people will make you feel a whole lot better than spending your time with a negative person. So why would you ever want to spend any of your time with a negative person?" - Mchezo Bwana

267. "It's better to ask if you can make a suggestion rather than voluntarily giving advice that wasn't asked for." - Mchezo Bwana

268. "Speak up for yourself. When you're confident expressing who you really are then you can truly be happy." - Mchezo Bwana

269. "Telling the truth is progress." - Mchezo Bwana

270. "Some people are like mannequins, so fake that they pretend to be real. They're capable of giving Oscar worthy performances sometimes." - Mchezo Bwana

271. "To meditate is to medicate." - Mchezo Bwana

272. "Failing is how you practice becoming successful." - Mchezo Bwana

273. "You're more likely to get lost following people that don't know how to get where you wanna go." - Mchezo Bwana

274. "If you want the world to be a better place, visualize what that would look like, make a commitment to self improvement, take action and help people." - Mchezo Bwana

275. "Practice is the process of improving." - Mchezo Bwana

276. "If you give a person an example to visualize they can picture what you're saying." - Mchezo Bwana

277. "Three of the rarest statements you'll ever hear are; I didn't know that, I made a mistake and I was wrong about that." - Mchezo Bwana

278. "Bad listeners have to be told the same thing over and over again." - Mchezo Bwana

279. "Sharing the best version of yourself with the world makes it a better place." - Mchezo Bwana

280. "Bullies just need to be punched in the mouth. Just be willing to fight. It doesn't matter if you win or not. People like to travel the path of least resistance. It wears a person out to know that they're always going to have to fight every time they see you. It's much easier for them to avoid you and look for someone else to mess with." - Mchezo Bwana

281. "Most people believe what they are told not what they've researched for themselves." - Mchezo Bwana

282. "When you get rejected yet you're still willing to continue making attempts, you develop confidence in your abilities and you'll eventually start to getting more yeses." - Mchezo Bwana

283. "When you speak less you avoid saying too much." - Mchezo Bwana

284. "You have to be willing to stand up for yourself and fight. To stand up for yourself is a victory." - Mchezo Bwana

285. "Some people are like junk food, they may look good, smell good, make you feel good and even taste good but they're not really good for you." - Mchezo Bwana

286. "If it's not a mutually beneficial relationship, I don't really see the benefit of continuing the relationship." - Mchezo Bwana

287. "Doing a favor can gain favor."- Mchezo Bwana

288. "Action, discipline, commitment and patience are the holy alliance of success." - Mchezo Bwana

289. "You don't prove how smart you are by trying to be right all the time you prove it by finding solutions to problems." - Mchezo Bwana

290. "You know it can be done if it has been done before. So that means that you can do it too. You wanna know how the successful people did it? Put in the time and effort to study them and you'll figure it out." - Mchezo Bwana

291. "Hang around people that know how to do things and there will be more opportunities for you to get things done." - Mchezo Bwana

292. "As you broaden your horizons your mind perceives more." - Mchezo Bwana

293. "To be aware is to know. To know gives you the ability to utilize." - Mchezo Bwana

294. "To win you need to study. Success requires discipline." - Mchezo Bwana

295. "Negative thoughts are the road block you must move past in order to reach true happiness." - Mchezo Bwana

296. "Signals and signs are a substitute for speech. Gestures communicate ideas and feelings." - Mchezo Bwana

297. "If you're not getting the desired results consider switching to a better strategy." - Mchezo Bwana

298. "To win you need to study. Success requires discipline." - Mchezo Bwana

298. "Listening is a learned skill." - Mchezo Bwana

299. "The follow up and the follow through are two very important things to do, especially in sells." - Mchezo Bwana

300. "Always remember you've got someone rooting for you." - Mchezo Bwana

www.ingramcontent.com/pod-product-compliance
Lightning Source LLC
Chambersburg PA
CBHW051958290426
44110CB00015B/2301